Transparency Masters
to Accompany
Fundamentals of Quality
Auditing

Transparency Masters to Accompany Fundamentals of Quality Auditing
B. Scott Parsowith

© 1995 by ASQC

10 9 8 7 6 5 4 3 2 1

ISBN 0-87389-240-2

Acquisitions Editor: Susan Westergard
Project Editor: Jeanne W. Bohn

ASQC Mission: To facilitate continuous improvement and increase customer satisfaction by identifying, communicating, and promoting the use of quality principles, concepts, and technologies; and thereby be recognized throughout the world as the leading authority on, and champion for, quality.

For a free copy of the ASQC Quality Press Publications Catalog, including ASQC membership information, call 800-248-1946.

Printed in the United States of America

 Printed on acid-free recycled paper

 ASQC
Quality Press
611 East Wisconsin Avenue
Milwaukee, Wisconsin 53202

To the memory of my parents,
Marty and Pearl,
and to my family:
Sandy, Roni, and Pam

Contents

Introduction

Chapter 1   Overview of Quality Auditing   1

Chapter 2   Audit Definitions and Applications   9

Chapter 3   Phase 1—Audit Initiation and Preparation   27

Chapter 4   Phase 2—Performance of an Audit: On-Site Evaluation   49

Chapter 5   Phases 3 and 4—Reporting and Closure Phases   67

Chapter 6   Establishing the Framework for an Audit Program   81

Chapter 7   The First Seven Elements of a Quality System   91

Chapter 8   The Second Seven Elements of a Quality System   121

Chapter 9   The Final Seven Elements of a Quality System   153

Chapter 10 Statistical Process Control   175

Chapter 11 Statistical Sampling for Auditing   183

Index   195

Introduction

The original idea for creating this book of transparency masters came as a result of the need for a training course by the Harrisburg Chapter of the American Society for Quality Control (ASQC). The course was meant for employees/companies who wanted to be better versed in quality auditing and take the Certified Quality Auditor (CQA) exam given by ASQC. At the time, I was teaching quality management for the Continuous Education Program at Penn State York.

In conjunction with the course need, the director of training for the Continuous Education Program at Penn State also felt that a Quality Auditing Certificate Program should be developed to meet the needs of the business community. In the process of developing this course, I generated a set of transparencies, which incorporated basic principles and techniques in the quality auditing field.

This book of transparency masters provides the instructor of quality auditing with basic principles and key learning points covered in my book, *Fundamentals of Quality Auditing*. The chapters contained here are sequenced in the same manner as the chapters in the book. The format of these transparency masters is versatile enough to use for training in either an academic environment or as part of the continuous quality improvement effort in the work environment where the intent is to give employees a better understanding of quality auditing.

The transparency masters, as does the book, *Fundamentals of Quality Auditing*, provide a means of imparting information on quality auditing principles to companies anticipating a quality audit. In addition, individuals preparing for the CQA exam may find this book helpful in highlighting key learning points relative to the body of knowledge that is currently covered in the exam. The transparency masters may also be used to enhance presentations at seminars, trade shows, and quality education courses.

Permission is hereby given for the use of the transparency masters to generate transparencies that will accommodate the specific needs for which they are intended. This permission does not apply to mass reproduction.

Audit Trademarks

> ➢ Quality auditing is an art and a science.

> ➢ Quality audits are snapshots in time.

> ➢ Quality audits should not be confrontations.

> ➢ Quality auditors investigate, verify, and confirm.

> ➢ The quality audit should be used as a tool for continuous quality improvement.

Auditor Knowledge

- ➤ Quality system requirements
- ➤ Product specifications
- ➤ Investigation techniques
- ➤ Sampling techniques
- ➤ Communication techniques

Auditor Traits

- ➤ Observant
- ➤ Honest
- ➤ Investigative
- ➤ Questioning
- ➤ Thorough
- ➤ Communicates well
- ➤ Adaptable
- ➤ Cooperative

In General, There Are Two Types of Quality Standards

➤ **System standards**

Examples

- ANSI/ISO/ASQC Q9000 standards
- MIL-Q-9858A

➤ **Product standards (specifications)**

Examples

- Chemical and physical property requirements
- Dimensional tolerances

Review and Verify Documentation, Implementation, and Effectiveness of

➢ Policy manuals

➢ Procedure manuals or directives

➢ Work instructions, drawings, etc.

➢ General quality system requirements

➢ Individual product specifications

Audits Can

> ➤ Enhance internal quality systems

> ➤ Be part of continuous quality improvement efforts

> ➤ Help establish trusting relationships internally and externally

Audits Are Not

➢ Acceptance of product

➢ Punch lists

➢ Public hangings

Chapter 2
Audit Definitions
and Applications

What Is an Audit?

➤ Quality audit definition per ANSI/ISO/ASQC Q10011-1-1994 "A systematic and independent examination to determine whether quality activities and related results comply with planned arrangements and whether these arrangements are implemented effectively and are suitable to achieve objectives."

➤ Quality Applications

- System audit

- Process audit

- Product audit

Additional Audit Terms

- Compliance audit
  - Compliance to standards
  - Review of processes
  - Review of data
- Operational audit
  - Time studies
  - Work studies
- Readiness review by internal management
  - ANSI/ISO/ASQC Q9000 review of system
  - Prior to OSHA evaluation
- Management review
  - Review of processes, procedures, and controls
- Survey
  - Comprehensive evaluation

System Audit Definition

A documented activity performed to verify, by examination and evaluation of objective evidence, that applicable elements of the quality system are appropriate and have been developed, documented, and effectively implemented in accordance and in conjunction with specified requirements.

—ANSI/ASQC Q-1-1986

Types of Audits

➤ Internal audits

- Management system audits
- Self-assessments
- Mini-self-assessments

➤ External audits

- Supplier audits
- Third-party audits

➤ System audits

- Verification that a quality system exists

(continued)

Types of Audits *(continued)*

- ➤ Process audits
  - Verification that process procedures exist, are correct, and are being followed
  - Verification that process procedures are followed under standard, rushed, and adverse conditions
- ➤ Product Audits
  - Reinspection of product
  - Verifies inspector capabilities and correct use of specifications

© 1995 by ASQC

Hierarchy of Audits

Survey

System audit

Process audit

Product audit

Characteristics of Audits

➤ Are independent of doer

- • Performed by a person not responsible for production or services in area being audited

➤ Have measurement criteria

- • Specifications (quality system requirements and product requirements)

- • Attribute data (go/no-go)

- • Variables data (actual measurements)

(continued)

Characteristics of Audits
(continued)

➤ Are performed by competent personnel

- Trained audit team members

➤ Are cost-effective

- Prevention of problems

➤ Are samples of the system

- Isolate one small moment in time.

- Like shining a spotlight on a forest of trees, and drawing a conclusion about all of the trees based on the appearance of the highlighted trees.

➤ Must be sure the sampling procedure is correct.

Two Types of Sample Process Errors

➢ Type I error (alpha error)

• We assume something is unacceptable when it is actually acceptable.

➢ Type II error (beta error)

• We assume something is acceptable when it is actually unacceptable.

Sample Consideration

➢ Sample size

➢ Sample amount

➢ Location of samples

➢ Sampling errors

Avoid using MIL-STD-105 E during audits, since it is based on a continuous series of lots.

Use of Audits

➤ Continuous improvement efforts
- Internal
- External

➤ Benchmarking

➤ Value-added suppliers

➤ Certification
- Internal (quality system)
- External (suppliers)

➤ Adherence to *Auditor Code of Ethics*

Note: Do not use audits alone to determine acceptance of product.

Why Audit?

- ➤ Competition
  - • External—We want to have low-cost, high-value suppliers.
  - • Internal—We want to verify that our systems are adequate and effective.

- ➤ Regulation
  - • Imposed by customers
  - • Self-imposed
  - • General quality standards or internal quality standards
  - • Federal or state regulations
  - • ISO standard, etc.

- ➤ Self-preservation to audit ourselves before someone audits us
  - • OSHA

Audits Improve Performance if They

➢ Meet management needs

  • Provide feedback

➢ Provide a forward look in time

  • Could predict where process controls or product measurements are needed

➢ Measure effectiveness and compliance to internal and external policy and contract requirements

Who Is the Client?

➢ There are at least three customers we must satisfy on each audit.

- Auditee

- Boss

- Buyer of the service (client)

What Managers Do

- ➤ Plan
- ➤ Do
- ➤ Check
  Audits address the "check" function of the cycle by checking and monitoring a system
- ➤ Act

Source: W. E. Deming, *Out of the Crisis* (Cambridge, Mass.: MIT Center for Advanced Engineering Study, 1986), 88–89.

Audit Administration

➤ Formal audit procedures

- Initiation and preparation at least 25% of auditors' time
  - Areas to be audited
  - Team composition and training
  - Notification of auditee
  - Checklist development
  - Transportation
- On-site audit performance approximately 50% of auditors' time
- Reporting and closure approximately 25% of auditors' time
  - Audit report
  - Audit records
  - Tracking and closure

Chapter 3
Phase 1—Audit Initiation and Preparation

Define the Objectives

> ➤ Why are we doing this?

> ➤ What type of audit are we to perform (system, process, or product)?

> ➤ What do our "customers" want?

Establish the Scope

> What are the boundaries within which we will look?

- Audit plan, time frame
- Facilities, organization, departments
- Product line
  - A supplier may have numerous product lines
- Process area
  - Geographic location
  - Product area
- Quality assurance system
- Product standards
- Effect of subsuppliers

Note: A preliminary visit may be necessary as a time saver before planning an audit.

Identify Standards

- ➤ Government/state regulations
  - • DoD and MIL Standards, FDA, OBRA, etc.
- ➤ Industry standards
  - • ASME, AWS, API, etc.
- ➤ Contract specifications
  - • MIL-Q-9858A, ANSI/ISO/ASQC Q9000 standards, etc.
- ➤ Company manuals
- ➤ Department procedures
- ➤ Process instructions

Define the Resources

➤ Team Composition

- Trained and qualified

- Knowledgeable of process to be audited (technical experience)

- Humanistic

- Adjust the number of audit team members to the scope of the audit.

➤ Team size

- One-person audits are an invitation to trouble, although they can be done.

(continued)

Define the Resources *(continued)*

- Balance is important, but more than six auditors is a mob.

➢ Length of the audit
A typical quality system audit requires between 1–5 days to complete.

  - Less than 500 employees: 1–3 days

  - 500–1000 employees: 4–5 days

Note: Employee population is defined as the number of employees working in the area to be covered by the scope of the audit, and may not necessarily include the total number of employees working at the facility.

Lead Auditor Responsibilities

➤ Prepare the audit plan

➤ Select the audit team (most cases)

➤ Brief the audit team

➤ Submit a report

Desirable Auditor Characteristics

➤ Knowledge of quality, product engineering, and procurement principles and practices

➤ Knowledge of requirements

➤ Knowledge of techniques

➤ Sound judgment/open-mindedness

➤ Patience

➤ Interest

➤ Tenacity (strength)

➤ Professional attitude/integrity

➤ Good listening skills

(continued)

Source: L. Marvin Johnson, *Quality Assurance Program Evaluation* (West Covina, Calif.: 1990), 43–47.

Desirable Auditor Characteristics *(continued)*

- ➤ Inquisitiveness
- ➤ Good verbal and written skills
- ➤ Analytical skills
- ➤ Honesty
- ➤ Ethics
- ➤ Diplomacy
- ➤ Discipline
- ➤ Good planning skills
- ➤ Experience
- ➤ Objectivity
- ➤ Empathy

Auditor Musts

➢ Knowledge of verification techniques

➢ Knowledge of standards

➢ Knowledge of sampling techniques

➢ Knowledge of human nature

➢ Knowledge of time management

Undesirable Auditor Characteristics

- ➢ Argumentative
- ➢ Opinionated
- ➢ Lazy
- ➢ Easily influenced
- ➢ Inflexible
- ➢ Impulsive—Jumps to conclusions
- ➢ Gullible
- ➢ Uncommunicative
- ➢ Devious
- ➢ Poor at planning
- ➢ Unprofessional
- ➢ Prescriptive

Source: L. Marvin Johnson, *Quality Assurance Program Evaluation* (West Covina, Calif.: 1990), 43–47.

Contact the Auditee

➢ Informal contact by team leader

- Date (firm but flexible)

- Purpose

- Scope

➢ Formal contact by letter or memo

- Time and date of audit

- Purpose

- Scope

(continued)

Contact the Auditee *(continued)*

- Activities to be audited
- Interfacing organizations
- Applicable quality requirements
- Identification of team members
- Preliminary schedule

Note: Review pertinent items with audit team.

Source: Allan J. Sayle, *Management Audits,* Second Edition (Great Britain: McGraw-Hill, 1988), 9.

Perform Desk Audit

➢ Review quality assurance documentation of auditee

➢ Determine what control systems are in place

➢ Review prior audits

➢ Investigate exemptions or waivers

➢ Review performance history

Understand the Process

➢ What are the controls of the system?

- Do a desk audit of the QA system.

    - Look at the QA policy Manual.

    - Look at the process and procedure manuals (as appropriate).

➢ What facts are available?

- Key variables identified

- Statistics used to monitor processes

➢ Where (who) are the facts?

➢ What is the product?

- An audit team member should be familiar with the product being audited.

Review History

- ➤ Prior audits
  - Verify that previous corrective actions have remained in effect.
  - Verify that strengths are still in place.
- ➤ Procurement
  - Files should be examined for any changes or exceptions the supplier has requested in the past.
- ➤ Customer feedback
  - Frequency and type of past problems should be evaluated.
  - Number of change orders or waiver requests should be checked.

Develop Checklists that Provide

➢ Structure

- Must define checklist before you do the audit.
- Brainstorm with audit team to develop checklist.

➢ Required coverage

- Not designed to stifle creativity.
- Use common sense regarding applicability.

➢ A communication document

➢ A place to record data

- Objective evidence is required for anything less than satisfactory.

➢ Help in time management (pace of audit)

Source: Nuclear Quality Systems Auditor Training Handbook, Second Edition (Milwaukee Wis.: ASQC Energy Division/ASQC Quality Press, 1986), 42, and Dennis Arter, *Quality Audits for Improved Performance* (ASQC Seminar, Clearwater, Fla., 1991), 7.

Checklists—Points to Consider

➤ Auditors can use

- Canned checklists
- Yes/no checklists (attributes)
- Rating checklists (variables)

➤ Things to consider when developing questions for a checklist are

- What is the process during standard operation?
- What is the process under rushed conditions?
- What is the process when there is a problem?

Source: Dennis Arter, *Quality Audits for Improved Performance,* Second Edition (Milwaukee, Wis.: ASQC Quality Press, 1994), 31–34.

Summary of the Preparation Phase

- ➤ Define the audit objective
- ➤ Establish the audit scope
- ➤ Allocate resources
- ➤ Contact the auditee
- ➤ Develop checklists
- ➤ Review history
- ➤ Understand the process and control systems

Source: Dennis Arter, *Quality Audits for Improved Performance*, Second Edition (Milwaukee, Wis.: ASQC Quality Press, 1994), 36.

Transparency Masters to Accompany *Fundamentals of Quality Auditing* **47**

Results of the Preparation Phase

➤ Audit plan

- Auditee, purpose, scope, activities to be audited, team, standards

➤ Checklist questions

➤ Items and reference location of each requirement

➤ Initial evaluation

- Based on documentation received
  - Desk audit
  - QA manual
  - Product performance (past audits)

➤ Plan for action

- Areas needing attention
- Items to be confirmed

Source: Dennis Arter, *Quality Audits for Improved Performance,* Second Edition (Milwaukee, Wis.: ASQC Quality Press, 1994), 36.

Chapter 4
Phase 2—Performance of an Audit: On-Site Evaluation

The Performance Phase

➢ Hold opening meeting

➢ Conduct on-site audit

➢ Review controls of quality system

➢ Verify that the system is working

  • Is it documented, implemented, and effective?

➢ Share information

The Opening Meeting

➤ Must have

- Entire audit team present
- Auditee's plant manager and staff

➤ Requires two-way communication

- Trade introductions
- Restate objectives
- Form initial impressions
- State areas of concern of auditor and auditee
- Settle logistics: conference room, telephone, hours of operation, lunch, etc.

➤ Should take no more than 30 minutes

(continued)

The Opening Meeting *(continued)*

- ➤ If needed: Allow 15-minute maximum for auditee to present quality system enhancements
- ➤ Distribute the checklist(s)
- ➤ Define the audit schedule
- ➤ Be on time

There Are Several Causes of Quality Issues

➢ Lack of top management support

➢ Lack of organization

➢ Lack of training

➢ Lack of discipline

➢ Lack of resources

➢ Lack of time

➢ Lack of teamwork

➢ Lack of knowledge

➢ Lack of consistency

Auditors should look for symptoms of these issues.

Source: Allan J. Sayle, *Management Audits,* Second Edition (Great Britain: McGraw-Hill, 1988), 1–5.

Evaluating the Information

Formal (documented) control systems

vs.

Informal (understood/verbal) control systems

➢ Does top management believe in quality and are these beliefs communicated throughout the organization?

➢ Is the control system used by management?

➢ Is the control system adequate?

• Are key quality variables identified?

➢ Is the control system working?

• How is it monitored?

Verification Methods

➤ Three primary methods used

- Tracing

- Corroboration

- Sampling (discussed in chapter 11)

Tracing Techniques

➤ Go with the flow

➤ Techniques of tracing

- Tracing of contract—Series of audits performed on a contract as the contract progresses

- Random auditing—Reviews without a pattern what is taking place in a process at time of audit

- Horizontal auditing

  - Backward—From the end of process (from order completion toward beginning)

  - Forward—From the beginning of process (from order receipt)

  - Middle—Backward or forward from some critical point in the process

(continued)

Tracing Techniques *(continued)*

- Vertical auditing—Reviews management layers for elements such as quality goals and quality communications

- Departmental traces—Reviews numerous quality elements within a department

- Element traces—Reviews a quality element in various departments

Source: Quality Management International, *Quality System Auditor Training Course*, (Exton, Penn.: QML, 1994), 4–7.

Corroboration

Because perceptions vary, a statement made during an interview is not a fact until it is corroborated by someone else or is verified by a document.

The facts must agree

- ➤ Two different auditors
- ➤ Two different records
- ➤ Two different interviews
  - Combinations of the above
- ➤ Tie conclusions to what is tangible
  - Qualitative
  - Quantitative
- ➤ Forms, records, and procedures

Audit Sampling

Trying to find the truth in a limited amount of time

> ➤ Estimation sampling

> ➤ Discovery sampling

> ➤ Acceptance sampling

> ➤ What to sample?
>
>   • Critical items or areas
>
>   – Important to the auditee, key quality variables/key operators
>
>   • Overloaded/stressed areas

> ➤ How to sample?
>
>   • Random sample
>
>   • Unbiased sample

> ➤ How much to sample?

(*Note:* Sampling is discussed in chapter 11.)

Five-Step Method for Effective Interviews

1. Put person at ease.

   - Your presence is threatening.

2. Explain your purpose.

   - Demonstrate competence.

   - Be aware, not an expert.

3. Utilize proper questioning techniques.

   - Ask open-ended questions.

   - Avoid leading questions that start with "I understand that you. . . ."

   - Use "pregnant pause."

   - Ask why five times (why, why, why, why, why).

   - Ask five w's (why, who, what, when, where) and a how.

(continued)

Five-Step Method for Effective Interviews *(continued)*

- Listen twice as much as you talk.

4. Analyze and verify what is said.

   - Believe a confession.

   - Verify a claim.

   - Write your notes out loud.

   - Don't keep secrets.

   - Be flexible—allow for additional information and discussion.

5. Explain your next step.

   - Conclude cordially.

   - Follow up.

Source: Dennis Arter, *Quality Audits for Improved Performance*, Second Edition (Milwaukee, Wis.: ASQC Quality, 1994), 43–47.

Chapter 5
Phases 3 and 4—Reporting and Closure Phases

Reporting Phase

➢ Informal report

- Exit meeting—approximately 60 minutes at completion of on-site investigation

➢ Formal report

- Aim to have written and distributed within two weeks after the audit

Both types of reports must be clear and precise.

➢ Statements of nonconformance contain

- Requirement

- Location

- Evidence

- Element of noncompliance

The Exit Meeting

➤ Must have exit meeting after completion of on-site investigation. Approximately 60 minutes should be allocated for this meeting.

➤ Limit attendance to managers of areas audited.
QA manager alone is unsatisfactory (may filter or distort).

➤ Present summary (lead auditor).
It is okay to agree to disagree.

(continued)

The Exit Meeting *(continued)*

➤ State that audit observations are produced from limited amount of audit samples of the entire process. Management should not only review the incident cited by the audit team, but also investigate the system.

➤ Lead auditor should read through all deficiencies first, then discuss audit details. Individual auditors clarify and respond to specific questions.

➤ Keep minutes of the meeting.

➤ Explain follow-up and corrective action response process.

Observations/Findings

Should

> ➤ Restate system's deficiencies as action items relating to the standards or expectations.

> ➤ Be practical—try to limit observations/findings to no more than six deficiencies per a given severity level (management overload).

> ➤ Be based on knowledge and objective evidence resulting from the audit.

Should not

> ➤ Require specific problem-solving actions (leads to malicious compliance).

> ➤ Be based on perceived bias or gut feelings (leads to lack of legitimacy and credibility).

Degree of Severity of Observations

➤ The report should order observations by their importance.

Tier 1—Most critical—conflict with contractual or procedural requirements.

- A systemic deficiency that adversely affects the quality of the product or service.

(continued)

Degree of Severity of Observations *(continued)*

Tier 2—Isolated observations in conflict with contractual or procedural requirements
- An observation that appears to be an isolated nonconformance and does not represent a system deficiency.

Tier 3—Concerns
- Observations that may not be part of the required quality system, but are considered worthy of further consideration.

Sources: Bethlehem Steel Corporation—QA Subcommittee and Purchasing, *Supplier Excellence Program*, Bethlehem, Penn.: Bethlehem Steel Corporation, 1–3; and Dennis Arter, "Quality Audits for Improved Performance," (ASQC seminar, Clearwater, Fla., 1991), 15, 18.

Content of the Formal Audit Report

Formal audit report from audit team to client should include

➤ Purpose and scope of the audit

➤ Participants' names

➤ Background information, such as standards used in performing audit

➤ Summary of results

➤ Identified weaknesses in order of importance

➤ Date and signature of lead auditor

Formal Audit Report Should Avoid

➢ Emotional words and phrases

➢ Bias and slanted viewpoint

➢ Nit-picking

➢ Underlining and other distracting graphics

➢ More than six items requiring action for a given severity level

The Closure Phase

➤ Auditee should have 30–45 days to respond with a plan of action.

➤ Auditee's corrective action plan is evaluated.

- Accept, reject, or take partial acceptance.

- Assess reasonable chance of success.

➤ Formally close corrected items and those not requiring reaudit.

➤ Those items requiring on-site verification are reaudited.

➤ Letter of closure is issued

➤ Documentation and letter of closure with original report are filed.

Corrective Action Plan

Auditee's responsibility
Four fundamentals of corrective action

- ➤ Find problems

- ➤ Fix problems

- ➤ Correct the root cause of problems

- ➤ Implement a system that evaluates effectiveness of corrective actions

Corrective action response should not

- ➤ Be a defense of status quo

- ➤ Address specific deficiency without investigating underlying root cause

Retention of Audit Documents

> ➤ Audit records should be maintained for at least one audit cycle for follow-up audits.

> ➤ System should be established by auditing function based on contractual or internal requirements.

Auditing Pitfalls to Avoid

➤ Inadequate planning and preparation for the audit

➤ Inadequate communication with auditee prior to the audit

➤ Lack of clearly defined scope

➤ Inadequate knowledge of standards

➤ Lack of properly trained auditors

➤ Prescriptive when evaluating corrective action responses

➤ Failure to reevaluate implemented corrective actions

Source: Dennis Arter, "Quality Audits for Improved Performance," (ASQC Seminar, Clearwater, Fla., 1991), 15, 18.

Chapter 6
Establishing the Framework for an Audit Program

Establishing the Framework for an Audit Program

➢ Upper management gives authority to establish audit function.

- Charter and policy established

➢ Audit administrator is assigned.

- QA manager
- Purchasing manager
- Other manager or designee

➢ Purpose and scope of program is established.

- Minimum compliance purposes
- Continuous quality purpose

➢ Management must be apprised of the value of audit program.

Note: Buy-in may not be a given.

© 1995 by ASQC

Factors of the Audit Program

➢ Management policies

➢ Customer requirements

➢ Company size

➢ Type of product/service

➢ Audit policy or charter

➢ Audit procedures, manuals, workbooks

➢ Staffing, training

➢ Audit records and retention

Source: James Thresh, *How to Conduct, Manage and Benefit from Effective Quality Audits Home Study Course* (White Plains, N.Y.: MGI Management Institute, 1984), 2–4.

Effective Audit Policy

- ➢ States objectives of management and audit program

- ➢ Is consistent

- ➢ Is flexible

- ➢ Is communicated throughout organization

- ➢ Is supported by processes and procedures

- ➢ Establishes audit function's independence

- ➢ Establishes authority

- ➢ Establishes ground rules

Source: James Thresh, *How to Conduct, Manage and Benefit from Effective Quality Audits Home Study Course* (White Plains, N.Y.: MGI Management Institute, 1984), 2–12.

Effective Audit Procedure

- ➢ Implements and supports organizational policy and objectives
- ➢ Flows logically
- ➢ Uses clear definitions
- ➢ Defines methods, tools, and documents to be used
- ➢ Describes alternative methods when more than one outcome is possible
- ➢ Uses simple language
- ➢ Uses auditor manual or workbook

General Principles to Administrating an Audit

➢ Objectivity

- Independence
- Attack problem, not people
- Avoid conflict
- Verify data

➢ Confidentiality

- Information should not be shared by auditor from company to company
  - Compliance
  - Noncompliance

Audit Staff

Staff members are selected on the basis of

➢ Experience

➢ Knowledge

➢ Communication skills

➢ Personal traits

➢ Judgment

Audit Staffing and Training

Training program includes

- ➤ Audit policies and procedures

- ➤ Auditing and quality standards

- ➤ Auditor training courses

- ➤ Auditor's manual (if required by audit program)

- ➤ On-the-job training

- ➤ Presentation skills

- ➤ Report writing

Source: James Thresh, *How to Conduct, Manage and Benefit from Effective Quality Audits Home Study Course* (White Plains, N.Y.: MGI Management Institute, 1984), 2–12.

Audit Records Retention Program

Established by audit organization

➢ Permanent records

- Notification letter
- Audit plan (if separate document)
- Preassessment questionnaire
- On-site audit/evaluation
- Working papers
- Audit report letter
- Closure letter
- Auditor training/qualification

(continued)

Audit Records Retention Program *(continued)*

- ➤ Nonpermanent records
  - Nonessential notes
  - Supporting documents
  - Additional correspondence
- ➤ Index of records established
- ➤ Retention timetable established

Chapter 7
The First Seven Elements
of a Quality System

Management Responsibility (Element 1)

Quality objectives

➤ Quality planning

- Identification of process controls

- Quality inspection points

➤ Fitness for use

- Established quality criteria

- Established inspection criteria

➤ Performance

- Measurement system

(continued)

Management Responsibility (Element 1) *(continued)*

➢ Reliability

- Established conformance and performance criteria

➢ Calculation and evaluation of cost

- Standard cost system

- Quality cost system

➢ Safety

- Provide a safe environment

Management Responsibility (Element 1)

Quality system

➤ Understandable and effective

- Allocation of people, money, and training for continuous improvement

➤ Satisfies requirements

- Meets or exceeds customer or contract requirements

➤ Values prevention more than detection

➤ Is explained in company quality policy manual

Management Responsibility (Element 1)

Review of the quality management system
- ➢ Planned review
  - Scheduled
  - Established criteria
- ➢ Reviewers
  - Independent
  - Competent

Quality System (Element 2)

Structure of the quality system

➢ Ultimate responsibility

- Authority

- Delegation

- Organization charts

- Type of organization

  - Military

  - Orthogonal
    (Refer to chapter 7 of *Fundamentals of Quality Auditing* for diagrams of these types)

(continued)

Quality System (Element 2) *(continued)*

➤ Lines of communication and interaction

- Monitoring
- Feedback

➤ Human factors

- Attitudes
- Training
- Resources and personnel
  - Hiring qualified personnel

Quality System (Element 2)

Documentation of the quality system

➤ Quality planning

- Short-term

- Long-term

- Quality projects

- Process controls

- Procedures and work instructions

➤ Maintenance of quality records

Contract Review (Element 3)

➢ Defined and documented requirements are reviewed.

➢ Capabilities exist that can meet contract requirements.

➢ Differences are resolved.

➢ Records of contract review are maintained.

Design Control (Element 4)

Specification and design input

➤ Translates

- Contract-to-manufacturing criteria
- User needs into production requirements

Produceability

- Manufacturing capabilities
- Transmittals

Design Control (Element 4)

Design planning

- ➤ Defined responsibilities
- ➤ Understandable technical outputs
- ➤ Standardization
  - • Similarities to standard products
- ➤ Quality requirements
  - • Acceptance criteria
  - • Statutory requirements

(continued)

Design Control
(Element 4) *(continued)*

- Maintainability
- Reliability
- Serviceability
- Performance criteria
- Conformance criteria
➢ Disposal of
  - Product
  - By-product

Design Control (Element 4)

Design product testing and measurement

- ➤ Test methods
- ➤ Tolerances/variables/attributes
- ➤ Equipment
  - Software
  - Hardware

Design Control (Element 4)

Design qualification and verification

- ➢ Evaluation
- ➢ Risk assessment
- ➢ Conformance/performance
- ➢ Operational conditions
- ➢ Validation of software/computer systems

Design Control (Element 4)

Design review and production release

➢ Management approval

➢ Customer approval

➢ Production release

- Is verified by appropriate documentation

Design Control (Element 4)

Market readiness review

➢ Documentation/availability

- Installation manuals

- Operation manuals

- Maintenance manuals

➢ Customer service

- Training of field personnel

➢ Availability of spare parts

Design Control (Element 4)

Design change control

➤ Baseline release

➤ Obsolete document control

➤ Change verification

Design Control (Element 4)

Design requalification

➢ Reevaluation

• Original or new requirements

➢ Process modifications

➢ Feedback analysis

Document Control (Element 5)

Generation of documents is controlled

➤ Process for writing

  • Policies, procedures, etc.

➤ Process for approval

  • Content approval

➤ Process for distribution

  • Sign-off sheets upon receipt of documents

  • Tally sheets of distribution

➤ Documents should be available at work locations.

Document Control (Element 5)

Revisions/distribution of documents are controlled.

> System for distribution

- Tally sheets of redistributions

Obsolete documents should be identified and removed.

Procurement (Element 6)

General

➤ Planning/control of the procurement of supplies or services

➤ Relationship with suppliers

- Short-term

- Long-term

➤ Feedback

➤ Potential suppliers evaluated for their ability to provide stated requirements

➤ Inquiries shown to potential suppliers

Procurement (Element 6)

Selection of qualified suppliers

➤ Demonstrated capability/reliability of supplier's system

➤ On-site assessment

- Review effectiveness of supplier's QA systems

- Process/product audits

➤ Evaluation of samples

- Submission of test samples

➤ Past history

- Product/service performance/conformance data

- Supplier commitment to quality

- Published experience of others

Procurement (Element 6)

Agreement on quality assurance parameters

➤ Records to be submitted

➤ Sampling

  • Inspection and test methods

➤ Types of inspection/verification methods

  • On-site

  • Receipt

➤ Periodic assessment or as needed

Procurement
(Element 6)

Purchase orders include

➤ Definition of requirements

- Quality system requirements
- Product tolerance specifications
- Quantities
- All requirements clearly stated

➤ Initial review for completeness

Procurement (Element 6)

Incoming inspection planning and control

➢ Adequate inspection planning such as

- 100% inspection
- Samplings plans

➢ Selection of characteristics

- Measured
- Evaluated for conformance

➢ Quarantined areas

Procurement (Element 6)

System to resolve quality disputes or noncompliances

- ➤ Channels of communication
  - Who are contacts?
  - Who has final say at supplier's facility?
  - Who are the authority figures?
- ➤ Routine and nonroutine occurrences
  - Waivers, etc.

Procurement (Element 6)

Receiving quality records

➤ Supplier performance assessments/test reports

➤ Trend analysis

➤ Identification/traceability

Customer/Purchaser-Supplied Product (Element 7)

Procedures that provide

➤ Verification

➤ Inventory control

➤ Security

➤ Storage

➤ Maintenance

➤ Reporting of damaged material

Chapter 8
The Second Seven Elements of a Quality System

The Second Seven Elements of a Quality System

8. Product identification and traceability

9. Process control

10. Inspection and testing

11. Inspection, measuring, and test equipment

12. Inspection and test status

13. Control of nonconforming product

14. Corrective and preventive action

Product Identification and Traceability (Element 8)

Provide a system that identifies product in accordance with procedures

- ➤ Methods of identification
    - Drawings
    - Documents
    - Bar codes
    - Computers
    - Tagging, painting, etc.
- ➤ Handling/processing
- ➤ Storage

(continued)

Process Control (Element 9) *(continued)*

➢ Documented work instructions, specifications, and drawings

➢ Equipment

  • Production

  • Measurement

➢ Flow diagrams

➢ Key variables identified

➢ Key variables measured and evaluated

Process Control (Element 9)

Process capability

- ➤ Process effectiveness

- ➤ Yields

- ➤ Quality costs

- ➤ Monitoring of product characteristics during production and installation

- ➤ Review of data

    - Control charts

    - Histograms

    - Trend analysis, etc.

- ➤ Decisions for adjustment of process based on data

Process Control (Element 9)

Environment—Impact production has on environment and impact environment has on production

> ➤ Water, air, power, chemicals

> ➤ Temperature

> ➤ Humidity

> ➤ Cleanliness

> ➤ Disposal

>> • Safety concerns

>> • Environmental concerns

> ➤ Regulations

Process Control (Element 9)

Equipment control and maintenance

- ➤ Approval prior to use
- ➤ Protection
  - • Winterizing
  - • Environmental
  - • Shutdown/lack of use
- ➤ Preventive maintenance
- ➤ Qualified repair personnel (monitoring of repairs)
  - • Trend analysis of repairs, etc.
- ➤ Computer authorizations

Process Control (Element 9)

Special processes

➤ Equipment accuracy, standardization, and variability

- Calibration

- Standardization

- Drift

➤ Type of tests or processes

- Nondestructive

    - Magnetic particle

    - Ultrasound

(continued)

Process Control (Element 9) *(continued)*

- – X-ray
- – Dye penetrant
- – Visual
- – Electronic
- – Eddy current
- Welding
- Brazing
- Chemical
- Biological

Process Control (Element 9)

Qualified personnel and tests performed during special processes must be verified.

➤ Operator capabilities and qualification must be kept.

➤ Certification records must be kept.

- Processes

- Equipment

- Personnel

(continued)

Process Control
(Element 9) *(continued)*

➤ Records of tests performed must be kept.

- Time, temperature, etc.
- Personnel performing tests
- Review of data
- Filing of results

➤ Special processes that cannot be verified after the fact must be monitored throughout the production process.

Workmanship meets product or service criteria performed during special processes.

Inspection and Testing (Element 10)

Incoming inspection of product

- ➤ Sampling plans
  - Documented
  - Implemented
  - Verified
- ➤ Certification
  - Requested
  - Verified
  - Retained
- ➤ Conformance to requirements
  - Verified
  - People responsible for decision

Inspection and Testing (Element 10)

In-process inspection

- ➤ Location of inspections
  - Planned
  - Documented
  - Implemented
- ➤ Frequency
  - Planned
  - Documented
  - Implemented, performed
- ➤ Status verification
  - Conformance to requirements indicated

(continued)

Inspection and Testing (Element 10) *(continued)*

➢ Verifications

- First-piece setup

  - Manual setup

  - Automatic equipment

- Conformance to requirement

  - Process

  - Product

➢ Personnel performing inspections are identified

  - Production personnel

  - QA personnel

  - Third party

Inspection and Testing (Element 10)

Final inspection and testing

➤ Acceptance inspection/tests

- 100% inspection

- Lot sampling

- Continuous sampling

- Random sampling

➤ Product auditing

- Continuous

- Periodic

- Random

(continued)

Inspection and Testing (Element 10) *(continued)*

➢ Nonconformance feedback

- In-house continuous improvement
- Customer notification

➢ Responsibility for decision

- Traceable
- Retrievable
- Maintained

Inspection and test records

- Recorded
- Maintained

Inspection, Measuring, and Test Equipment (Element 11)

Measurement control

- ➤ Calibration specifications (written)

- ➤ Types of calibration machinery

- ➤ Calibration standards (used for comparisons)

- ➤ Personnel trained in metrology techniques

  - • What tools to use

  - • How to use tools

  - • When to use tools

(continued)

Inspection, Measuring, and Test Equipment (Element 11) *(continued)*

➤ Devices used for acceptance of product

- Process control tools
- Final inspection tools

➤ Control of environment

- Temperature
- Humidity, etc.

➤ Repeatability, confidence studies

Inspection, Measuring, and Test Equipment (Element 11)

Standardization/calibration control

- ➢ Standardization

- ➢ Calibration

- ➢ Recalibration

  - • Recall of material, if needed

- ➢ Procedures/work instructions

  - • How to standardize/calibrate

  - • Frequency of standardization/calibration

  - • How to measure

(continued)

Inspection, Measuring, and Test Equipment (Element 11) *(continued)*

➢ Document evidence of calibrations

➢ Identification and traceability

- Location of use

- Serial number

- Record of gages used to measure materials

➢ Trend analysis

➢ Where purchase of calibration service is required, organization is accredited

Inspection, Measuring, and Test Equipment (Element 11)

Record retention

➤ Standardization

➤ Calibration

➤ Procedures/work instructions

➤ Retrievability

    • Timetable for records retention

Inspection and Test Status (Element 12)

Status of material maintained throughout process

- ➤ Paper records
- ➤ Computer records
- ➤ Product tags
- ➤ Bar codes
- ➤ Traceability of product with releases

Identification of responsible personnel for conformance decisions

- ➤ Records of product release

Control of Nonconforming Product (Element 13)

Identification

- ➤ Marking
- ➤ Tagging
- ➤ Computer identification

Control of Nonconforming Product (Element 13)

Segregation to prevent inadvertent use

> ➤ Physical

> ➤ Records

> ➤ Computer

Control of Nonconforming Product (Element 13)

Disposition

➢ Disposition evaluation by authorized personnel

➢ Classification

- Repair

- Rework

- Reapplication

- Recall

- Referral

- Scrap

(continued)

Control of Nonconforming Product (Element 13) *(continued)*

➤ Reevaluation

- Repair
- Reapplied
- Scrap

➤ Reclassification

➤ Documentation

- Forms
- Reports
- Approvals
- Referral to customer

Corrective and Preventive Action (Element 14)

Identification of problem

- ➤ Causes
  - Common
  - Special
  - Repeat/trends
  - Isolated incidents
- ➤ Analysis of problems
  - Root-cause determination
  - Evaluation of impact
    - Costs
    - Performance
    - Safety
    - Customer satisfaction

Corrective and Preventive Action
(Element 14)

Implementation of corrective actions

- ➤ Initiation of corrective actions

    - Short-term actions

    - Long-term actions

- ➤ Changes required

    - Process

    - Product

    - Specification

    - Quality systems

    - Work instructions

(continued)

Corrective and Preventive Action (Element 14) *(continued)*

- ➤ Responsibility for follow-up
  - Personnel
- ➤ Recording of changes made to prevent recurrence
  - Process
  - Procedures
- ➤ Review and monitoring of changes to analyze effectiveness of corrective actions

Implementation of preventive actions

- ➤ Initiation of preventive actions
- ➤ Evaluation of preventive actions

Handling, Storage, Packaging, Preservation, and Delivery (Element 15)

Packaging
- ➤ Prevent damage
- ➤ Maintain identification
- ➤ Conform to requirements

Preservation
- ➤ Protection from deterioration

(continued)

Handling, Storage, Packaging, Preservation, and Delivery (Element 15) *(continued)*

Delivery

➤ Protection of quality of product after final inspection

- In-house
- Loading
- During shipment
- Upon shipment

➤ Feedback system for damaged goods upon receipt

Quality Records (Element 16)

Examples of quality records

- ➤ Procedures
- ➤ Production criteria
    - Setup
    - Changes
    - Specifications
- ➤ Test data
- ➤ Qualification data/records
- ➤ Process control data/records
- ➤ Audit reports
- ➤ Performance data/records
- ➤ Calibration data/records

Quality Records (Element 16)

Identification

➢ Traceable to product or process

  • Legible

  • Dates

  • Time

  • Turn/shift

  • Personnel responsible for data collection

Collection

➢ System

➢ Personnel responsible

Quality Records (Element 16)

Indexing

➢ Recall process

➢ Specified period of retention

- Retrievable

- Storage

- Disposal

  – Yearly

  – Monthly, etc.

Quality Records (Element 16)

Storage status

➤ Type of storage

- File cabinets
- Microfiche
- Computer disks

➤ Type of environment

- Minimize deterioration
- Controlled environment
- Prevent loss
    - Water damage
    - Fire damage, etc.

(continued)

Training of Personnel (Element 18)

Training is provided.

➤ Location and time to train

- Classroom

- On-the-job experience

➤ Evaluation of classes and teachers

- Internal

- External

Training of Personnel (Element 18)

Employee training is verified.

- ➤ Requalification or recertification is performed
- ➤ Qualification/certification on the basis of
  - Education
  - Training
  - Experience
  - Evaluation of skills verified
- ➤ Training records are maintained.

Training of Personnel (Element 18)

Human factors are considered.

> ➤ Inspire continuous improvement.
>   - Understand responsibility
>   - Motivate
> ➤ Be knowledgeable about quality.
>   - Company importance
>   - Individual importance
>   - Quality awareness
> ➤ Provide a good work environment.
>   - Individual performance
>   - Team performance
>   - Recognition

Servicing (Element 19)

Servicing of products or services to meet specified requirements

> ➤ Activities performed to written procedures

- Assembly instruction

- Additional/spare parts lists

- Service numbers

- Service activities to verify that contract requirements are met

- Instructions

    - Usage

    - Maintenance

Servicing (Element 19)

Liability

- ➤ Warranty
  - Claims
  - Traceability
- ➤ Ability to recall
  - Records
  - Designs
  - Specifications
  - Process controls
  - Results of testing
  - Review of other materials involved
  - Maintenance

Servicing (Element 19)

Safety

➤ Risks

- Material safety data sheets

➤ Direct usage of product

➤ Indirect usage of product

➤ Labels

- Instructions

- Warnings

Quality Cost Analysis (Element 21)

Standard cost system

Cost of nonconformance

Quality costs system

- ➤ Prevention

- ➤ Appraisal

- ➤ Internal failure

- ➤ External failure

Chapter 10
Statistical Process Control

Key Process and Product Variables

Process map (flowchart)

- ➤ Identification of
  - Quality control points
  - Locations of activities
  - Authority responsible for performance of activities
  - Numbering conventions coordination
- ➤ Comparison to external and internal customer requirements (quality plan)
- ➤ Process and inspection data feedback to control system

Variability of Processes and Products

Causes of variability in processes

- ➤ Human resources
- ➤ Machines
- ➤ Methods
- ➤ Materials
- ➤ Environment

Evaluation of the causes of variability

- ➤ Special causes
- ➤ Common causes

Source: W. Edwards Deming, *Out of the Crisis* (Cambridge, Mass.: MIT Center for Advanced Engineering Study, 1986), 310–12.

Statistical Control Charts and Process Stability

> ➤ Statistical limits (based on past data)

> ➤ Statistical control

> ➤ Data points outside control limits

> ➤ Data points exhibiting patterns

> ➤ Determination of special causes or process changes

Control Limits and Control Charting Risk

Incorrect assessments of conclusions based on data

- ➤ Type I error—alpha (producer's risk)
  - Conclude process is out of control when it is actually in control.
- ➤ Type II error—beta (consumer's risk)
  - Conclude process is in control when it is actually out of control.

Correct assessments of conclusions based on data

- ➤ Process is in control when it is actually in control.
- ➤ Process is out of control when it is actually out of control.

Types of Data Collection

Variables

➤ Measurement

Attributes

➤ Count

Note: It is important to know what type of data is collected.

Variables Data Control Charts

➤ X-bar, *R* control charts

➤ Out of control signals or patterns

- Data points that are beyond the control limits

- Data points in a run configuration

- Data points in a trend configuration

- Data points in a periodic configuration

- Data points in a stratified configuration

Attributes Data Control Charts

➢ Nonconforming products
  - p charts
  - np charts
➢ Nonconformities per unit
  - c charts
  - u charts

Chapter 11
Statistical Sampling for Auditing

Aspects of Sampling

➤ Sampling obtains information from a part of the total population or field

➤ What type, how much, and when to use sampling techniques requires the use of scientific principles and common sense.

➤ Sampling is used in

- Accounting

- Business

- Industry

- Quality auditing

Methods Employed Must Suit Needs of Audit

Types of approaches

> ➤ Estimation sampling

> ➤ Discovery sampling

> ➤ Acceptance sampling

> > • Is based on a continuous process and is not suggested for use in quality audits

Estimation Sampling

A random number of samples is taken from the field and the amount of nonconformances contained in the sample is counted.

- ➤ Answers the question, "How many or how much?"

- ➤ Provides estimation of frequency of occurrences of an event within the field.

- ➤ Provides range of sampling error (precision/point estimates).

Source: Herbert Arkin, *Handbook of Sampling for Auditing and Accounting,* Third Edition (Englewood Cliffs, N.J.: Prentice Hall, 1984), 13–14.

Considerations While Using Estimation Sampling

➢ Sample precision

➢ Confidence level

➢ Risk of making improper assessment

How to Attain Sample Size for Estimation Sampling

- ➢ Establish sample precision.

- ➢ Establish confidence level.

- ➢ Estimate the maximum rate of occurrence.

- ➢ Determine field size.

- ➢ Refer to sample size table (appendix D of *Fundamentals of Quality Auditing*) for correct sample size at particular confidence. Results will estimate nonconformance rate.

Source: Herbert Arkin, *Handbook of Sampling for Auditing and Accounting,* Third Edition (Englewood Cliffs, N.J.: Prentice Hall, 1984), 89.

Discovery Sampling

➢ Is a fastidious method of sampling.

➢ Discloses needle-in-a-haystack situation.

➢ Provides assurance at a prescribed confidence level of disclosing at least one nonconformance within a given field.

➢ Is not to be used to determine percentage of occurrence.

Source: Herbert Arkin, *Handbook of Sampling for Auditing and Accounting,* Third Edition (Englewood Cliffs, N.J.: Prentice Hall, 1984), 134.

How to Attain Sample Size in Discovery Sampling

➤ Establish the probability level required.

➤ Estimate occurrence rate.

➤ Determine field size.

➤ Refer to sample size table (appendix E in *Fundamentals of Quality Auditing*) for correct sample size.

Sample Selection

Establish what is to be sampled depending on the scope of the audit

> ➤ Critical work instructions

> ➤ Highly stressed, high-volume, high-precision areas

> ➤ Contributory factors that make the process successful

How Much to Sample

- ➤ Sampling approach
- ➤ Desired confidence level
- ➤ Time allocated
- ➤ Type of assessment (attributes vs. variables)
- ➤ Scope of audit

How to Select an Unbiased Sample

➤ Equal chance of selection

➤ After process is running consistently

➤ Selection of predetermined number of random samples

  • Use of random number tables

  • Use of calculator

Index

Acceptance sampling, 185
Alpha error, 18, 179
ANSI/ISO/ASQC Q10011-1-1994, 10
ANSI/ISO/ASQC Q9000 standards, 5, 11
Attributes, 180
Attributes data control charts, 182
Audit(s)
    administration of, 25, 86
    approaches in, 185
    briefing auditee during, 64
    characteristics of, 16–17
    data collection during, 60–61
    definition of, 10
    desk, 42
    effective procedures in, 85
    external, 13
    hierarchy of, 15
    impact on performance, 22
    internal, 13
    initiation phase of, 28
    items covered in plan for, 29
    noncharacteristics of, 8
    objectives of, 30
    pitfalls to avoid, 79
    process, 14
    product, 14
    purpose of, 7
    reasons for, 21
    retention of documents in, 78
    supplier, 13
    system, 13
    third-party, 13
    types of, 13–14
    use of, 20
Auditee, 40–41
    briefing of, during audit, 64
Auditor
    desirable characteristics of, 36–37
    knowledge of, 3

    musts of, 38
    team meetings for, 65
    traits of, 4
    undesirable characteristics of, 39
Audit program
    establishing framework for, 82
    factors of, 83
    policy, 84
Audit records retention program, 89–90
Audit sampling, 59
Audit staff
    skills of, 87
    training of, 88
Audit trademarks, 2

Backward auditing, 56
Benchmarking, 20
Beta error, 18, 179

c charts, 182
Certification, 20
Checklists, 45–46
Client, identifying, 23
Closure phase, 76
Compliance audit, 11
Confidentiality, 86
Continuous improvement efforts, 20
Contract review, 92, 101
Contract specifications, 32
Control limits and control charting risk, 179
Control of nonconforming product, 122, 145–48
Control system, 43
Corrective action plan, 77
Corrective action, 122, 149–51
Corroboration, 55, 58
Customer feedback, 44
Customer/purchaser-supplied product, 92, 120

Data collection
  during audit, 60–61
  types of, 180
Departmental traces, 57
Design change control, 109
Design control, 92, 102–10
Design planning, 103–4
Design product testing and measurement, 105
Design requalification, 110
Design review and production release, 107
Desk audit, 42
Discovery sampling, 185, 189–90
Document control, 92

Element traces, 57
Estimation sampling, 185, 186–88
Exit meeting, 68, 69–70
External audits, 13

Formal audit report, 68
  content of, 74
  elements to be avoided in, 75
Formal control systems, 54
Forward auditing, 56

Government/state regulations, 32

Handling, storage, packaging, preservation,
  and delivery, 155–57
Horizontal auditing, 56

Incoming inspection planning and control, 117
Industry standards, 32
Informal control systems, 54
Informal report, 68
Inspection, measuring, and test equipment,
  122, 139–44
Inspection and testing, 122, 134–38, 144
Internal audits, 13, 163–64
Interviews, five-step method for effective,
  62–63

Key variables, 43, 176

Lead auditor, responsibilities of, 35

Management responsibility, 92, 93–97
Management review, 11
Management system audits, 13

Managers, role of, 24
Market readiness review, 108
MIL-Q-9858, 5
MIL-STD-105 E, 19
Mini-self-assessment, 13

Nonconforming product, 145
np charts, 182

Objectivity, 86
Observations, 71
  degree of severity of, 72–73
On-site evaluation, 49–65
Opening meeting, 51–52
Operational audit, 11

p charts, 182
Performance, impact of audits on, 22
Performance phase, 50
Preparation phase, 29–47
  results of, 48
Preventive action, 122, 149–51
Prior audits, 44
Process audit, 10, 14
Process control, 122, 125–33
Procurement, 44, 92, 113–19
Produceability, 102
Product audit, 10, 14
Product identification and traceability, 122,
  123–24
Product standards, 5
Purchase orders, 116

Quality auditing, 2
Quality cost analysis, 174
Quality issues, causes of, 53
Quality records, 158–62
Quality standards, types of, 5
Quality system, 92, 98–100, 122
  contract review, 92, 101
  control of nonconforming products, 122
  corrective and preventive action, 122,
    149–51
  customer/purchaser-supplied product, 92,
    120
  design control, 92, 102–10
  document control, 92
  handling, storage, packaging, preservation,
    and delivery, 155–57

Quality system—*continued*
inspection, measuring, and test equipment, 122, 139–44
inspection and testing, 122, 134–38
inspection and test status, 122, 144
internal quality audits, 163–64
management responsibility, 92, 93–97
process control, 122, 125–33
procurement, 92, 113–19
product identification and traceability, 122, 123–24
quality system, 98–100
servicing, 169–71
training of personnel, 165–68

Random auditing, 56
R control charts, 181
Reporting phase, 68
Resources, 33–34
Review and verification, 6
Review history, 44

Sample
selecting unbiased, 193
size of, 192
Sample process errors, types of, 18
Sample selection, 191
Sampling, 55
applications of, 184
discovery, 189–90
estimation, 186–88
Scope, 31
Self-assessment, 13
Servicing, 169–71
Specification and design input, 102
Standards, identifying, 32
Statements of nonconformance, 68
Statistical and analytical techniques, 172–73
Statistical control charts and process stability, 178
Statistical process control, 175
control limits and control charting risk, 179

key process and product variables, 176
sample selection, 191
statistical control charts and process stability, 178
variability of processes and product control, 177
Supplier audits, 13
Survey, 11
System audit, 10, 12, 13
System standards, 5

Team meeting, 65
Third-party audits, 13
Time studies, 11
Tracing
departmental, 57
element, 57
Tracing, 55, 56–57
Training, audits, 88
Type I error, 18, 179
Type II error, 18, 179

u charts, 182
Use of audits, 20

Variability of processes and products control, 177
Variables, 180
Variables data control charts, 181
Verification, 6
Verification methods, 55
audit sampling, 59
corroboration, 55, 58
sampling, 55
tracing, 55
tracing techniques, 56–57
Vertical auditing, 57

Work studies, 11

$\bar{x}$ charts, 181